What Is a Tornado?

Robin Johnson

 Crabtree Publishing Company
www.crabtreebooks.com

Author: Robin Johnson

Publishing plan research and development: Reagan Miller

Editors: Reagan Miller and Kathy Middleton

Proofreader: Janine Deschenes

Design and photo research: Samara Parent

Prepress technician: Samara Parent

Print and production coordinator: Katherine Berti

Photographs
iStock: p4; p6; p11; p15; p16
Shutterstock: p8 © Alexey Stiop; p19 © littleny
Thinkstock: p18
Wikimedia Commons: p12 © VORTEX II/NOAA ; p13 © Daniel
    Schwen; pp20-21 © Justin Hobson

All other images from Shutterstock

About the author
Robin Johnson has written more than 60 educational books for children. She plans to keep writing books and chasing rainbows—whatever the weather.

Library and Archives Canada Cataloguing in Publication

Johnson, Robin (Robin R.), author
        What is a tornado? / Robin Johnson.

(Severe weather close-up)
Includes index.
Issued in print and electronic formats.
ISBN 978-0-7787-2423-0 (bound).--ISBN 978-0-7787-2438-4
(paperback).--ISBN 978-1-4271-1753-3 (html)

        1. Tornadoes--Juvenile literature. I. Title.

QC955.2.J65 2016   j551.55'3   C2015-908686-8
                                         C2015-908687-6

Library of Congress Cataloging-in-Publication Data

CIP available at the Library of Congress

Crabtree Publishing Company

www.crabtreebooks.com   1-800-387-7650

Printed in Canada/032016/EF20160210

Published in Canada
Crabtree Publishing
616 Welland Ave.
St. Catharines, Ontario
L2M 5V6

Published in the United States
Crabtree Publishing
PMB 59051
350 Fifth Avenue, 59th Floor
New York, New York 10118

Published in the United Kingdom
Crabtree Publishing
Maritime House
Basin Road North, Hove
BN41 1WR

Published in Australia
Crabtree Publishing
3 Charles Street
Coburg North
VIC 3058

Contents

Changing weather

Wind is moving air. It blows our hair and spins our toys.

Each day brings us different **weather**. Weather is what the air and sky are like in a certain place at a certain time. Sunlight, clouds, rain, and **wind** are all parts of weather. Sometimes, the weather is nice outside. You can twirl and dance in the sunlight. A gentle breeze turns your pinwheel.

Stormy weather

At other times, the weather is not nice at all. The wind howls and blows. Dark clouds fill the sky. Rain falls and makes puddles on the ground. Periods of bad weather are called **storms**. You play inside during storms. You can go outside again when the storms are over.

Thunderstorms

Some storms have strong winds, heavy rain, bright **lightning**, and booming **thunder**. Lightning is a flash of **electricity** in the sky. Thunder is the sound that lightning makes when it moves through the air. Storms with lightning and thunder are called **thunderstorms**

*Tornadoes form from **funnel clouds**. A funnel cloud is a cone-shaped tunnel of spinning wind.*

funnel cloud

Tornadoes

Big thunderstorms can make **tornadoes**. A tornado is a huge, spinning tower of wind that stretches from a storm cloud down to the ground. It forms when warm, wet air meets cool, dry air. The warm and cool air press against each other and start to spin. This spinning air forms a funnel cloud. The cloud keeps turning and growing downward. When it touches the ground, it becomes a tornado.

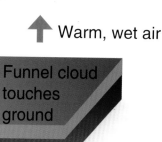

Wind spinning

Cool, dry air

Warm, wet air

Funnel cloud touches ground

What do you ThinK?

Tornadoes are sometimes called "twisters." Why do you think they are called that?

High-speed storms

The winds of a tornado spin at very high speeds. As it spins, the tornado moves along the ground, destroying everything in its path. A tornado can rip up tall trees. It can damage houses and other buildings. Some tornadoes can even lift heavy objects, such as cars and trucks, into the air!

It is very dangerous to be outside during a tornado. Strong winds hurl branches, doors, glass, and other **debris** through the air.

Severe weather

Tornadoes are a type of **severe weather**. Severe weather is dangerous. It can hurt people and animals. It can damage buildings and land. Most tornadoes last for only a few minutes, but they can do a lot of damage in a very short time. It is important to learn how you can stay safe during these powerful storms (see page 14).

Many tornadoes look dark gray or black because they pick up dust and debris as they move across the ground.

9

Tornado Alley

Tornadoes can happen almost anywhere in the world. Some places get many more tornadoes than others. An area called **Tornado Alley** lies in the middle of the United States. This is where warm, wet air moving up from the Gulf of Mexico meets cool, dry air moving down from Canada. Dangerous storms form where they meet. Tornado Alley gets hundreds of tornadoes each year.

Texas, Oklahoma, Kansas, and Nebraska are some of the states in Tornado Alley.

Tornado Alley

Tornado season

Tornadoes can happen in any month and at any time of the day. However, they usually happen during warm weather, so they are most common in spring and summer. **Tornado season**, which is the period when most tornadoes happen, lasts from March to July each year. Tornadoes usually occur in the late afternoon or early evening, after the Sun has had many hours to warm the air.

What do you ThinK?

Why are there so many tornadoes in Tornado Alley each year?

Storm trackers

Meteorologists watch tornadoes and other storms as they form. Meteorologists are scientists who study weather. They measure the wind, **temperature**, and other parts of tornadoes. They use this information to try to **predict** where and when tornadoes will form, as well as what path they will follow. They warn us about tornadoes as early as possible so that we have time to get to safe places before the storms reach us.

Tornadoes are very hard to predict because they can form without much warning and change their direction suddenly. New weather tools are helping meteorologists predict tornadoes sooner than ever before, however.

Watches and warnings

Meteorologists report information about tornadoes on television, on the radio, and online. A **tornado watch** means there is a chance that tornadoes might form in the area. People are told to get ready for the storm and check for updates. A **tornado warning** means a tornado has been seen in the area. People are told to hurry to safe places right away.

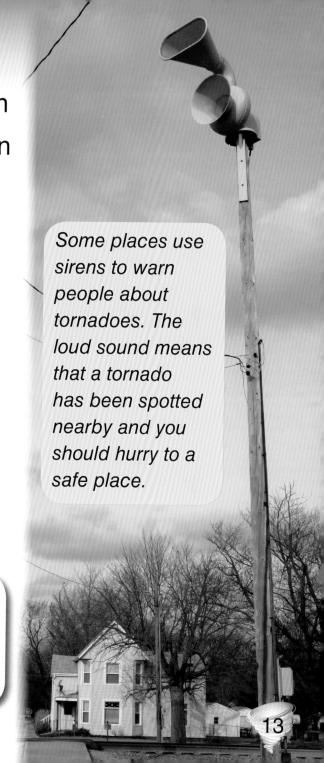

Some places use sirens to warn people about tornadoes. The loud sound means that a tornado has been spotted nearby and you should hurry to a safe place.

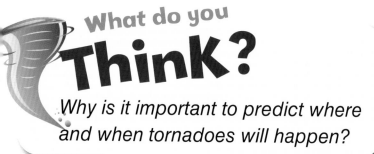

What do you Think?

Why is it important to predict where and when tornadoes will happen?

Safe places

If there is a tornado warning where you live, hurry to your basement or **storm shelter**. A storm shelter is a room built under the ground away from buildings. If you do not have a basement or storm shelter, go to the lowest floor of your home. Keep away from windows because strong winds could break the glass.

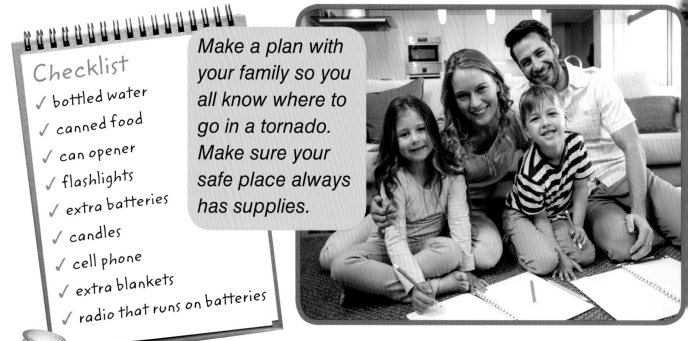

Checklist
- ✓ bottled water
- ✓ canned food
- ✓ can opener
- ✓ flashlights
- ✓ extra batteries
- ✓ candles
- ✓ cell phone
- ✓ extra blankets
- ✓ radio that runs on batteries

Make a plan with your family so you all know where to go in a tornado. Make sure your safe place always has supplies.

Take cover

Take cover inside a bathroom, closet, hallway, or under a stairway in the middle of your home. Stay away from the building's outside walls. They could be damaged by trees and other large objects. Climb inside an empty bathtub or crawl under a heavy table or desk. They will help protect you from flying or falling debris. Crouch down and cover your head with your hands.

Remember to take your pets with you to a safe place if you have time to do so.

TORNADO SHELTER

15

Go inside

Most tornadoes happen without much warning. If you are outside when a tornado siren sounds, you can still stay safe. Go inside your house, school, or other strong building nearby. Buildings made of brick or **concrete** are stronger and safer than those made of wood.

Mobile homes and cars are not safe places during tornadoes. Strong winds can lift them right off the ground!

Go low

If you cannot get indoors in time, do not try to outrun the tornado. Instead, lie down on the ground in a ditch or other low area of land. Lie flat on your stomach with your hands over your head. Keep away from trees and cars because they could be thrown by the wind. Do not take cover under bridges because they could fall down and crush you.

You may not see tornadoes coming, but you will hear them! These storms are very loud. They sound like a hundred speeding trains!

What do you Think?

During a tornado, would you be safer inside a wooden barn or a brick house? Explain your thinking.

17

After the storm

Before going outside, check a weather report to make sure the tornado is over. It is a good idea to keep a battery-powered radio in your safe space so you can hear a weather report even if you lose power during the storm.

TORNADO SHELTER

After the storm, there may be debris all around. Sharp nails, broken glass, and other items could hurt you. Stay inside until adults have cleaned up the debris and it is safer to go outside.

Check on your family and friends after a storm. They may need help or a place to stay.

Keep out!

Stay out of houses and other buildings that have been damaged by the storm. Roofs, walls, or other parts of buildings could fall down at any time. Do not touch **power lines** that have fallen to the ground. Electricity may still be flowing through them and you could be seriously hurt. Also, keep away from areas that have **flooded**, or filled with water, from heavy rain.

Tornado test

Take this quiz to see how much you have learned about tornado safety. Point to the answer you think is right for each question. Read the book again to find the information you need. The correct answers are shown on the next page.

1. Before meteorologists warn you about tornadoes, you should...

a) make a tornado plan and prepare a kit with useful supplies

b) do nothing because you do not live in Tornado Alley

2. If you hear a tornado warning when you are inside, you should...

a) go to your basement or underground storm shelter right away

b) keep playing your video game because the storm will soon pass

3. If you do not have a basement or storm shelter, you should...

a) look out an upstairs window to see which way the tornado is coming

b) go to the lowest floor of your home and stay away from windows

4. If you see a funnel cloud or tornado when you are outside, you should...

a) hurry inside a strong building, or if you cannot find one, lie on your stomach on the ground

b) try to outrun the tornado because you are a really fast runner

5. After a tornado, you should...

a) rush to your best friend's house to make sure she is okay

b) wait for an adult to tell you the storm is over and it is safe to go outside

Picture this

Check your answers to the tornado test below. Then make a tornado safety poster! Use words and pictures to show one safety tip you learned in this book.

Answers

1. a) Tornadoes can happen almost anywhere, so you should always be ready for them.

2. a) Under the ground is the safest place to be during these powerful storms.

3. b) Stay away from windows because broken glass and flying debris could hurt you.

4. a) Even the fastest people and cars cannot outrun these high-speed storms.

5. b) Check on your friends after adults check the weather report and clean up debris.

Learning more

Books

Changing Weather: Storms by Kelley MacAulay and Bobbie Kalman. Crabtree Publishing Company, 2006.

How Do Tornadoes Form? And Other Questions Kids Have About Weather by Suzanne Slade. Picture Window Books, 2011.

What is wind? by Robin Johnson. Crabtree Publishing Company, 2013.

Websites

This useful fact sheet tells you what to do before, during, and after a tornado:
www.ready.gov/kids/know-the-facts/tornado

Learn all about tornadoes and other severe weather at:
www.nssl.noaa.gov/education/svrwx101/tornadoes/

Learn about tornadoes and other dangerous storms at this weather website:
http://stormchasing101.weebly.com/tornadoes.html

Be a weather whiz kid and learn more about tornadoes at:
www.weatherwizkids.com/weather-tornado.htm

Be weather-wise and answer Liz the Weatherlizard's questions at this fun website:
www.scholastic.com/magicschoolbus/games/weather/index.htm

Words to know

Note: Some boldfaced words are defined where they appear in the book.

concrete (KON-kreet) noun A strong, hard, stonelike material used for building

debris (duh-BREE) noun Pieces of broken or wrecked objects

electricity (ih-lek-TRIS-i-tee) noun A form of energy found in nature that can also be made by people

funnel cloud (FUHN-l kloud) noun A spinning, cone-shaped tower of wind that stretches down from a storm cloud but does not touch the ground

power lines (POU-er lahynz) noun A metal line, or cable, that is used to carry electricity from one place to another

predict (pri-DIKT) verb To tell what will happen before it takes place

severe weather (suh-VEER WETH-er) adjective, noun Dangerous weather that can cause damage and hurt people and animals

temperature (TEHM-per-a-chur) noun A measure of how hot or cold something is

tornado (tawr-NEY-doh) noun A fast-spinning tower of wind that stretches from a thunderstorm cloud and touches the ground

Tornado Alley (tawr-NEY-doh AL-ee) noun An area in the middle of the United States where many tornadoes occur

A noun is a person, place, or thing. A verb is an action word that tells you what someone or something does. An adjective is a word that tells you what something is like.

Index